OVERTIME IS SO OVER

AOS Publishing
New York, NY

Copyright © 2015 by Ashley Sutton
Originally written 2010

All rights reserved.
Published in the United States of America by
AOS Publishing, New York

ISBN 0-9981662-0-0
First Edition
Library of Congress Control Number: 2016916117

Illustrations by Jane Gardner, janegardnerdesign.com

Press Inquiries: Press@OvertimeIsSoOver.com

www.OvertimeIsSoOver.com

OVERTIME IS SO OVER

Leave the Office and Get Your Life Back!

Ashley Sutton and J.C. Curry

New York

THIS BOOK IS DEDICATED
TO ALL OF THE LATE
NIGHTS AT THE DESK, THE
"NOT-SO HAPPY" HAPPY
HOURS, AND ALL
OF THE TV-BINGING THAT
WE MISSED.

CONTENTS

1 GETTING YOUR LIFE BACK (1)
   There are 24 hours in a day; you just spent 18 of them at work. What is this life?

2 THE TRUTH ABOUT OVERTIME (15)
   Why you're actually diminishing your salary when you work late

3 MYTHS THEY'D LIKE YOU TO BELIEVE (29)
   7 signs you'll be duped into late night purgatory

4 MAYBE IT'S YOU (45)
   C'mon, you didn't think you were perfect did you?

5 YOU: THE BUSINESS (63)
   Most businesses have open and closing hours…why not employees?

6 INVEST IN YOURSELF (91)
   Change your mindset, and you'll change the game

7 EXCEPTIONS TO THE RULE (109)
   Don't get carried away, sometimes you'll need to suck it up and stay late

8 THE END GAME (121)
   Know your worth, and work like you know it

1

GETTING YOUR LIFE BACK

We all want to be champions in the workplace. We've never heard of anyone *wanting* to be a loser…have you? At some point, we've all thought long and hard about the next project we'll conquer, what extra work we'll take on, or even the next all-nighter we'll pull, just to make sure our "great" work gets noticed, and will someday pay off, right?

Not necessarily; if anyone honestly thinks that any of these pipe dreams will propel into that dream promotion, you may as well prepare the tombstone effective immediately. Despite what you may have been taught, it's not always about working until you can't work anymore. Burnout, lack of motivation, and loss of overall happiness become the price you pay when you overexert yourself.

Only you know your worth, and until you figure it out, you'll continue to work aimlessly. They say "time is money," but time is just that…time. There are only 24 hours in a day; you decide how you will spend them, because there's always a choice.

You're probably wondering why you should even bother listening to us. Let's just say, we've been there. I, Ashley, had the pleasure and opportunity to work at a Fortune 500 company in New York City, probably the most competitive city in the United States. As a recent college graduate, I was under the impression that the more overtime I put in, the more projects I took on, and the more I said "yes," the more I would grow and get ahead. Little did I know that this "theory" couldn't have been further from the truth. All that happened was that I became demotivated and tired. I dreaded going into the office. As a fresh grad, I'd gone from the dorm room to the boardroom in a matter of weeks, and all I knew was that it was time to take a leap. In my first job, my role and focus was systems work. I set out to master every single computer system and become more efficient at it. I was excited about this new role because I wanted to learn and grow with a company that was an industry leader.

During the first month or so, I became acclimated to organizational processes, and things were going smoothly. Once I got my feet a little wet, I started flying solo. As I became much more familiar with the role, I led weekly development milestone meetings, created and distributed weekly sales reports, created new solutions for managing schedules, collaborated with packaging designers and engineers to develop the product's look and feel. I even became the "go-to" person for many of the product development inquiries, systems requests, and project management issues.

It was exciting, I won't lie— that is, until requests started piling in that could have easily been handled by the requestor. I started to see that on occassion, some co-workers would automatically pile on work, before they even tried to resolve an issue on their own. I continued to say yes and help out, even when requests weren't even from my department, or even my function. Why? I wanted it to be known that I was a team player and would get it done no matter the cost.

Several months went by, and I realized the

price I'd been paying was my free time. Every night by the time I looked up, I was leaving the office at 10 and 11 o'clock, sometimes midnight. It became very unhealthy; not to mention I was walking the streets of NYC late at night. I wasn't making enough money to hop in a taxi every night.

Eventually I realized that many of my late nights were my fault, for two reasons:

1. I wasn't efficient with my time at work, and wasn't prioritizing the right items

2. I didn't understand the value of "no," so I allowed people to take advantage; I didn't understand the value of my time.

Often, I used to plan out my work schedule for the day and allocate time to each of my tasks, but it felt like so much on my plate that I didn't know where to start. So, I tried to work through every task— and there went my schedule. Let's not forget the distractions. I would drop what I was working on, leaving it unfinished so I could help out. At the time, I thought it was the right thing to do because I was helping the collective team. Then, I became so overwhelmed and began producing incomplete projects and missing deadlines. I wasn't an efficient team player, and I wasn't even efficient in my own role. No one was to blame but me.

At the end of the day those projects of mine weren't delivered on, because of my fear of saying no and lack of prioritizing. It didn't mean that I wasn't the right person for the job, but my mentality to push through, and desire not to let anyone down, led me down a path of no return.

Yearning to be a team player made me want to get every bit of the work done, but no matter how many projects or tasks I followed through on, more kept coming. I had no idea how to prioritize, and was too nervous to ask my manager for help.

I started to take a look at my productivity and realized that it was on the decline. I kept telling myself that since I was fresh off of the graduation stage, I could handle a few long nights at work. I'd sure pulled my share of all-nighters for final exams in college. There's only one small tidbit I forgot to realize with this bright idea… as soon as I'd finish my studying, I would walk across campus, and hop into my cozy bed! Now, not only was I staying late at work, but I was commuting late, and arriving home late. The cycle of waking up early and doing it all over again and again, continued.

Inevitably, my late nights at work began taking a toll. I was dragging in the morning and started coming into the office late, a pattern that did not go unnoticed by my managers.

Arriving to work late was unacceptable, and it ate into my productive time at work. So I was super tired and unproductive, plus it was simply unprofessional. My whole day would go down the drain because I was unprepared mentally. When you are working a demanding job and trying to maintain balance in your life, it can become stressful. You need to make sure you leave at a decent time at the end of the day. Otherwise, you'll start to see a decline your performance—take it from me.

One day, I looked around and noticed that a few co-workers did leave at a reasonable time and, yes, without their laptops. And they were leaving with a few items on the agenda that weren't fully wrapped up. I'd been at the company for about 6 months at this point, and figured my learning curve should have been closing in. I began to ask myself, "why is there an expectation that the rest of the team stay and work long hours?" That was the wrong question. Nobody forced me to stay late.

While it may have been *implied* that the work needed to get done, there were no parameters set. There's always a choice.

I started to evaluate and separate the critical items from the items that truly could wait until the next day. I'd built myself into a work machine. When people requested something, I made sure that it got done that day. That may be a great work ethic, in theory, but it's counterproductive when you put off projects of a higher priority in order to help someone else's day go smoothly. After a bit of struggle, I learned to start asking the right questions. Questions such as, "what's the timeline?" or "what items should we look to deprioritize, in order to make room for this hot item?" While these questions seem like no-brainers, for a newbie like myself, it wasn't always crystal clear.

Realizing that I had to get over wondering if

someone would be upset with me for not being able to execute a same-day systems request was the happiest day; especially requests that could be done the next day or even the next week. Immediately I went on a personal strike against staying late every night. I remember one co-worker laughing in disbelief the first time I leaned over and said "have a good night, I'll see ya tomorrow" at 7:45. It seemed radical to leave before 8:00.

Once I began valuing my time, I felt a sense of freedom and never looked back. My team members didn't respect me any less because of my newfound work behaviors; in fact, I think it was just the opposite. I kept a great rapport with my team and maintained a healthy lifestyle.

I figured, I couldn't be the only one dealing with this stress, and as it turned out, co-author J.C. was also feeling the same strain and drain. So, we decided to pour our experiences into this book, in hopes that we could help at least one person feeling the stress of working grueling hours. This book is meant to be a guide for changing your mindset and your method of working, if you find yourself overworking (and not living). Pointless overtime is a serious addiction that most Americans have suffered from at some point in their career. We urge you to apply the lessons learned in this book to your situation. We hope you will see increased productivity and reduced stress. More importantly, we want you to get your life back.

Now, let's get on with it. Have you experienced any of these scenarios?

- You stay at work until 9:30 or 10:00 at night to finish a report, and the next day you are greeted by your manager who is more concerned with the color of the font in your report, than its content.
- You miss out on your Great Aunt Fan-

ny's 90th birthday because of an assignment marked "URGENT, URGENT, must be completed Today!" So you take one for the team and stay late, only to discover later that you'd been given a fake deadline… two weeks early!
- You pretty much never take a lunch break. Instead you check emails, edit reports, pull data, check voicemails, and answer every phone call…all while eating your lunch.

If you answered "yes" to any of the above or have experienced something similar, you're about to experience light at the end of the tunnel—and no, it's not a train headed straight toward you! We've been where you are, and it's not a good feeling. If you are at this point, we're glad you're reading this book. We had enough of the chaos, and I'm sure you have, too. So, let's leave the desk mentality behind, and start valuing ourselves… because Overtime is so OVER!

Let's Get Started!

NORMAL *vs* **OVERTIME**

2

THE TRUTH ABOUT OVERTIME

So what is the matter with salaried employees working overtime, anyway? Everyone you know is putting in extra hours, so shouldn't you be, too?

There are a number of people who would say yes. They believe that putting in extra unpaid hours is something that comes with having a career and, what's worse, that you won't be successful unless you do.

We used to think that, too, but now we think it's nonsense. Let's go through a couple of reasons why.

Number one: There are a number of factors that play into one's success, including one's discipline, willingness to put in hard work, efficiency, and passion. We guarantee you that those who have achieved a certain level of success didn't get there just by working overtime, if they had to work overtime at all.

Number two: "Success" is a very complex and subjective idea. It's unique to each and every individual and it must be defined by that individual, if she/he hopes to ever achieve it. Once a person has defined *success*, she/he can then begin to plot out the steps needed to reach that goal; whether or not overtime is included in that process is dependent on the goal.

We're not here to tell you that working overtime won't help you at all in your career. Nobody ever explained what working in corporate America could be like, and the concept of working late nights was certainly not an open book. We'd like to share with you the hard-earned truths we've learned about putting in all those extra hours.

The Deathly Truth

The Japanese have a great word to describe the idea of overtime: *Karoshi*, which literally means "death from overwork." It dates back to 1969, when a 29-year-old male worker at one of Japan's top newspapers dropped dead. Many other young, seemingly healthy laborers, as well as corporate executives, began dying of strokes or heart attacks without any prior history of illness. It was believed that the real cause of death was stress from overwork.

During 1985, a study was developed by Marianna Virtanen, M.D. The study on white-collar workers found that people who worked more than 10 hours a day had a 56 percent increased risk of heart disease, heart attack, or death.

So, would you like to know what you are getting in exchange for all this generous overtime that you have been providing your company? You got it: an early death sentence. Perhaps we're being a tad bit melodramatic here, but the point is that overtime really does take its toll on your health over time. But it's not just because you are spending more time dealing with stressful issues on the job. You also *stop* living the part of your life that offers you a release from work. When you spend evening hours in the office trying to catch up on work or finish projects, you are neglecting vital and essential social time and downtime. You don't get to do Happy Hour with your friends, and you have no time for family. Such outlets allow us the opportunity to think about other things, to talk about plans, to re-evaluate life, to laugh and joke and smile, even to vent about everything that's been going on at work. Without social time, you will never be able to effectively deal with the stress that comes with working.

Additionally, you find that you don't have time for yourself. You'll be too tired when you get home after a 10 or 12-hour day to do much more than grab something to eat, shower, and hit the bed only to wake up the next morning and do it all again. You haven't given your mind any real break from work because you haven't had the chance to deprogram yourself from your day. Repeating these habits becomes a regimen. After a while you'll find yourself living to work, instead of working to live.

The Happy Truth

Forbes magazine, one of our favorite sources for interesting lists, shared a survey conducted in 2013 on happiness, in which it ranked countries around the world in the order of places where people were happiest. Are you surprised to learn that the United States did not make the top ten?

There are certainly a number of factors that contribute to this ranking, but of the countries ranking higher than the United States on the list, the top seem to have a few things in common: happiness and balance over long hours. In the case of Denmark, the full-time work week averages 37 hours. The United States Department of Labor, under the Fair Labor Standards Act, doesn't precisely define what "full-time" work means in terms of hours. In fact, according to the website, "there is no limit on the number of hours employees 16 years or older may work in any workweek." Hours worked are left up to the employer to decide. So in effect, "full-time" work in the United States could constitute 40 hours a week or 70 hours a week or anywhere the employer decides is enough.

The result? Americans work the longest number of hours of all industrialized countries, according to the International Labor Organization. It's no wonder the US doesn't top the list of happy countries. How can it be happy if all we do is work?

Life is not meant to be lived inside a 4-by-4 cubicle—or in a grand corner office, for that matter. It is not meant to be lived working hard day in and day out without any reward for the extra effort. Sadly, this is what work has become for many people in America today: a daily grind of more and more work, more and more time spent at work with little to no time to spend doing the things we love most, the things that bring us happiness. And what's more, we have stopped living to fulfill our own dreams and started living to fulfill the dreams of the companies for which we work.

The Helpful Truth

Let's dive into a little story about two friends who graduated from college and started working at the same time. Dick graduated from college and got an awesome job as a day trader for a financial institution making $75,000 per year. Jane also landed an awesome job as a financial analyst for an oil and gas company, making $50,000 per year.

Dick is expected to be at work before the market opens each day at 8:00 in the morning (EST-- even though he lives in a CST time zone) and doesn't leave work until well after the market closes. This is largely due to the fact that he has to spend time researching companies and making predictions about what the market may do the next day. So he starts work before 7 in the morning, and doesn't usually leave the office until 7:00 o'clock at night.

Jane is expected to be at work when the office doors open at 8:00 in the morning. and leaves when everyone else does, around 5:00 in the evening. She doesn't usually doesn't need to stay late.

But here's the kicker, Dick and Jane actually make the same amount of money. How is that possible? Well, if you take his salary and divide it by the number of hours per year he works and then do the same for Jane, you will arrive at the same number! It would appear that Dick should make $36.06 per hour and Jane should make $24.03 per hour, but because Dick works more than 40 hours a week, he ends up making the same as Jane.

Actually, Jane has the potential to make more money than Dick by taking on a second job or starting her own side business, which she has time to do, because she's not at her desk every night until 7.

When you work overtime for your company on a consistent basis, you end up devaluing your labor, your time, and your salary! While this sucks for you, it's great for your company. As you devalue your labor, time, and salary for yourself, you increase your company's return on investment for you as an asset. Dick's financial institution is getting him for 60 hours per week at the 40-hour-per-week price! It's a steal for his employer, as it is for yours when you decide you are going to give away your work for free.

The Never-ending Truth!

One of the terrible things about working overtime is that once you start doing it, you begin to set a level of expectation that is hard to change. Dick works 60 hours per week and is devaluing his labor, but he is also increasing the level of productivity that his manager has come to expect from him in a work week.

Let's say Dick can typically accomplish the following tasks in a 40-hour work week (using a simple example):

- Create 5 trade reports
- Research 10 stocks

Since Dick's manager has now given him more work to do, consequently, he's now really working 60 hours a week (although his manager doesn't realize this), and accomplishes the following tasks:

- Created 10 trade reports
- Researched 15 stocks

Obviously, Dick's manager is going to be much happier with the 10 trade reports and research on 15 stocks, so now he assigns Dick to do this every week! Dick has unfortunately set an expectation that is going to be difficult to change without making himself look incompetent. Managing expectations is critical in this situation.

The Deflating Production Truth

A software developer from Houston is a hard worker and one of the brightest in his field. He works for a software company and wants nothing more than to help it be successful. He was hired to work 40 hours per week and asked to assist in the development of the company's core product, which we will call Product A. Of course, he wants to do a great job and get a lot accomplished in a day, but he quickly realizes that 40 hours a week is just not enough time to complete the production of Product A; he needs to work longer and harder to get the software finished in time for the sales department to have something to sell their customer and prospects. So he begins staying late, day by day, eventually ending up working 70 hours per week, even though he was only being paid to work 40. Over the course of two months, he was able to finally finish Product A. His total work time was 280 hours; his total work time as understood by the company was 160 hours. That's more than 100 hours of work for free!

Because the software company doesn't realize this, if the nice developer ever decides to hire someone else who won't be as generous with their time, the company will not have a realistic expectation of how much time and money really need to be allocated to complete the project on time and within the scope of the budget. The true cost of production remains unknown to the company because of false pretenses. Both the employer and the employee are now in a lose-lose situation.

While you might not care about what overtime does to your company, you should certainly care about what it does to you. Nobody is going to care more about you than you.

Now that we've defined overtime, the following chapters are designed to help you identify, navigate and mitigate the chaos.

3

MYTHS THEY'D LIKE YOU TO BELIEVE

Now that we've uncovered some truths about the overtime trap, let's take a look at 7 common business concepts and determine what they are *really* saying.

More Technology = More Flexibility

Have you ever been in a job where you looked up one day and said to yourself, "This isn't what I signed up for"? Did you ever regret talking yourself into this position because everything seemed "so right"? Before you accept any job, make sure you don't get seduced by all the bells and whistles.

See the offer letter below, as an example of what you really signed up for...

[Dear Sir/Madam:
Welcome to the XYZ Corporation; we offer great pay, unparalleled benefits, growth, and most importantly, flexibility. We even throw in a laptop and the most high-tech smartphone on the market to help you achieve work-life balance!

What do we mean by flexibility? You don't always want to lug around that company laptop, do you? Well, it's your lucky day; we also offer up a 20 percent discount on your phone bill when you sign up for the company smartphone plan. Seriously, no strings attached. Yes, we mean YOU, the employee, get to check your company email, review 3-year strategies, and prep for upcoming presentations all while filling up at the gas station, waiting for the subway, or even while sipping on a glass of red wine—all from the comfort of your phone! Yep, that's right... there's an app for that.]

Please beware of the fine print. Do you see it? Who are they kidding? The whole laptop/smartphone combo is a 2 for 1 deal because laptops and smartphones are designed to alert you to work situations, no matter where you are in the world. And what is "work-life balance"? There's no such thing when you have a laptop or any device that keeps you constantly updated on work. It is inevitable that work will sometimes cross its way into your personal life, and vice versa. But learn when to draw the line so you can stay sane. Trust us... there's no app for that!

Doing More Will Get You More

One of the first things they teach you in business school is that hard work will eventually pay off for you. They teach you to do more, go the extra mile, put in extra hours—on the assumption that if you do, you will get ahead faster. There are two reasons why this won't work. First of all, if they're teaching this to everybody in business schools across the nation, how will anyone have a competitive advantage over the next person to get ahead? The norm will essentially become "doing more," meaning you won't be doing more than anyone else. Second, there are a lot of people who work extremely hard and never get anywhere. Doesn't that tell you something? It's not just about how hard you work, but how *smart* you work.

People Will Notice When You Work Late
There is a common misconception that if you stay late at work, someone high up in your organization like your manager or your manager's manager will notice and will remember it when it's time for a promotion. This is a myth. Many times, when you are working late, the

person you're trying to impress is long gone. Who is going to see exactly what time you left? Probably nobody. And if nobody sees it, it didn't really happen; and therefore it won't count toward your brownie points with your manager and it won't help you get ahead.

There Is No "I" in TEAM

Ever notice how often teachers wanted students to put their heads together, and work in groups? We are taught this in an effort to help us get acclimated to working with others in groups and teams for the rest of our lives, particularly in our careers.

Don't get us wrong, working in groups is a fun way to continue to develop professionally. We just have a few precautions. Now, we have all heard the saying that there is no "I" in team and yet, we all know just how untrue it is. When you enter the real world, there are no teams; it's you trying to keep your job and get ahead! In the real world, more often than not, people fall short of producing their deliverables on time for the "team."

When you have a major project that has a critical deadline, there may that one person on your team who just can't get the job done on time. If you're on their team, their inability to deliver will be *your* fault, too. You'll end up trying to cover for them and take care of their responsibilities in addition to yours. If their job doesn't get done, you will take the blame, and if the job does get done, you won't get any credit. How's that for teamwork?

Ladies and gentlemen, there may be no "I" in team, but there isn't a "we" in team, either. There is an "I" in win; however, and if you want to win at work, then it's best to understand the team goals and figure out how you are going to work to achieve them.

One of the best ways to ensure you can meet your goals is to stay connected to your team and do regular check-ins. While one could simply say that we're all adults, and should be able to keep up with deadlines, that's not entirely a fair statement. Part of staying connected to your team is making sure that everyone understands the ask, has the bandwidth to perform the ask, and feels a part of the team. Happy and efficient teams often get the job done, and are able to excel above and beyond expectations. Teamwork makes the dream work.

Great Performance Review = Promotion Time!

It's that time of year again—time for your performance review. Time for you to meet with your manager and show him or her what a great job you did for the company this year. And of course, everybody knows that if you get a great performance review, you are going to get the

promotion you've been waiting for…right?

Wrong!

Getting a great performance review is not the only factor you need to get that promotion you've been dreaming of. Sure, you have worked harder, longer, and in general more than every other potential candidate in the office, but you still won't get that promotion. Why? Because, in some cases, you have done your job so well that they can't imagine losing you to another team that may have room in the budget to promote you.

Say you own a million-dollar mansion and need a little help keeping it clean. You have several positions in maintenance, including one for a housekeeper, a gardener, a pool serviceman, and a grounds manager. Let's just say that your housekeeper is the best in the world. He folds your sheets a certain way, keeps your floors so clean you could eat off of them, and knows how to iron clothes better than any dry cleaner. Now assuming all of this, would you ever consider promoting him to Grounds Manager? Probably not in this particular moment because there's no one to replace him. If you do your job so well that people can't imagine anyone else doing it, then you could find yourself deadlocked. Of course this scenario is a bit of a heightened example, as there are many reasons for why you may or may not be getting promoted (budget, headcount, capability, organizational shifts, etc). Never stop doing good work, just make sure you're covering other bases to stay top of mind for that desired promotion.

You'll Always Be Acknowledged for Your Work

When you were in grade school, your teacher was probably a stickler for making sure that the right person got credit for the work that they did. They even taught you about how plagiarism was wrong because you should never take credit for work that someone else did.
Unfortunately, most grade school children grew up to be your co-workers and now take credit

for things they didn't do. It happens all the time in the workplace. For example, a friend of ours used to work for a mid-sized software company where one of her lead salespeople never sold anything but was always taking credit for other people's sales. He'd say how he'd helped so-and-so close this deal, how he had brought so-and-so that deal, and would make public broadcasts about his "teamwork" via an email blast to almost the entire company. He'd even get commission checks from other people's deals! That was until the day he tried to take credit for a deal brought in by the V.P of sales. That ended up being his last day taking credit for someone else's work at that company—and his last day with the company.

This guy got away, for a long time, with taking credit for work he simply did not do. He isn't the only person in the history of the world to do it, and you probably know somebody just like him in your own company. The sad truth is that you will not always get acknowledged for the work you do. Sometimes someone else will take credit for it; other times the work will simply be taken for granted. Either way, don't assume that people are going to high-five you after your great work. Guess what, that's okay. It's not always about getting credit for every single thing. Learn when to make it count, and when to just let it go.

Mimic Your Co-Workers If You Want to Get Ahead

Acclimate, don't replicate. When we first meet someone, we as humans begin the process of evaluating them by observing them. We observe how they walk and talk, how they dress and present themselves, and whether they are humorous, serious, friendly, or reserved. We can also begin to determine, based on these observations, where that someone may fit into our lives as a friend, an associate, a lover, or just a general passerby. But one thing is for certain:

we wouldn't be able to determine any of this without observation; it is the foundation onto which good analysis and appropriate action are built.

This concept must be applied at work, and it should preferably happen early on. Getting hired to do your dream job is an amazing feeling, and of course you're anxious to do a great job; thus you act as a sponge, wanting to soak up everything to make sure you perform accordingly. When you first come aboard, you typically gauge the work culture and behavior. It's only natural to begin "mirroring" the work styles and actions of your team members. However, you must take the time in the beginning make observations. You may even start by asking a few basic questions like:

- What seems to be the work style in this department?
- Do my team members work late? How often?

- What are my team leader's or manager's expectations of me in this role, and can I fulfill them in a timely manner?

These are just some of the questions that you may want to ask while making your observations. The answers to these questions will give you a good indication of what your work life is going to be like, which will help you decide how to better assess your work style.

Let's look at Brian and Nick. Brian was hired as an account manager at a leading advertising agency. As part of the on-boarding process, he shadowed fellow account manager Nick for a month. They both share the same responsibilities and have similar working experiences. Brian notices Nick usually stays late every night "getting things done." Since Nick is a top account manager, Brian starts thinking this is normal behavior, and that he better jump on the bandwagon and start staying later if he wants to be at the top! Brian also notices that every time he passes Nick's desk, Nick is talking on his cell phone, texting, or playing online games. It then becomes apparent to Brian that Nick isn't a top manager because he stays late working "so hard." He stays late because he can't get his work done during normal work hours.

It's all fine and dandy to get acclimated with your new position, but there's a fine line between *acclimation* and *replication*. If you find that you have a more efficient way of working than someone who's been doing the job a long time, don't feel as though you're not a hard worker or that you don't want to be as successful as your counterparts. It simply means that you've found your own work style. Don't ever let a co-worker make you feel bad for leaving at a decent hour, especially if you know you've had a productive day.

Before we move on, please accept our apologies if you held any of these 7 myths dear to your heart. We hate to burst your bubble, but in many cases the very same tips and tricks that you pick up from your co-workers, read in that trusty-dusty employee handbook, or even hear straight from your supervisor can actually harm your overall productivity.

4

MAYBE IT'S YOU

It's easy to see how your manager could be the one to blame for your late nights in the office, and certainly supervisors and other coworkers play an important role—we'll get to them later. First you need to take a close look at *yourself.*

No one knows you like you. Be honest with yourself, and figure out what's keeping you at work so late. Ask yourself if your manager, for example, is truly the cause of your endless work day, or could it be that *you* don't know how to prioritize?

Most people think they work efficiently, but being productive is a true skill, one that takes practice to perfect.

Have you ever felt that you accomplished a million objectives in one day, only to realize that you didn't finish the one major thing you wanted to get done? You were too busy checking off all the *trivial* tasks on your to-do list. We all create the lofty "To-Do" list that's chock-full of faux tasks.

First, it's important to delineate the difference between a task and an objective. A *task* is a definite piece of work, whereas an *objective* is something that you intend to accomplish with a purpose. Responding to emails, returning phone calls, and attending meetings do not constitute as achieving an objective. They are only steps toward the objective, and only the objective itself really matters.

Efficient Is as Efficient Does

How many of us know the difference between *productivity* and *efficiency*? When you're productive, you deliver results. When you're efficient, you deliver those results without wasting resources, such as time or money.

If you'd like to run a self-check on your efficiency, start with these tricks of the trade:

Make a Reasonable To-Do List

Have you ever heard the phrase "don't bite off more than you can chew"? This also applies to your work habits. No one wants to leave work undone, but there's only so much you can take on in a day.

A daily to-do list should consist of items you can *actually* achieve that day. Try to limit your list to a maximum of 5-8 key items. Don't try to get sneaky and add 15 million subcategories to each item that really don't relate to your overall goal or objective!

Always Plan Ahead

If you know that you're responsible for delivering a biweekly report, make sure you give yourself ample time to perform all the steps leading up to it. Take Amy for example. She's a retail sales manager. Every two weeks Amy is responsible for reporting customer returns. Upper management typically wants to see the number of returns, in addition to reasons why they returned and any next steps or processes to put in place so as to minimize the number of returns in the future.

Since Amy knows this report is due every two weeks, there are some elements she can build into her report well before it's due. While Amy may not know the total number of returns a week before her deadline, she does know which in-store promotions and sales are currently running. She can also take a look at the previous year's gift receipt sales to determine the average number of returns that were a gift purchase. Taking a look at the previous year's concept roll-out could also be a great way to gauge the current year's designs, pricing, and advertising versus the previous year. All of the above could help Amy build assumptions for her report. There will be changes as the deadline approaches, but at least she will have a starting point and can focus on delivering a well thought-out report once she has all of her inputs. Always a good idea to be proactive rather than reactive when it comes to projects and deadlines.

Schedule/Attend Productive Meetings
For crying out loud, please don't hold meetings just for the sake of holding meetings. Always have a clear, concise agenda….and FOLLOW IT! Even if you aren't the meeting coordinator or leader, don't be afraid to keep your team on track and focused. Yes, some people may look

at you sideways and think to themselves "who invited the meeting patrol?" That's okay, let them get upset; meanwhile you just got a proverbial pat on the back from your manager.

We've all probably been in a meeting or two (or twenty) where we're supposed to discuss a certain project, and 10 minutes into the meeting it shifted into a totally different subject. Or five different side conversations were going on. Your co-workers are secretly thinking the same thing you're wondering, but alas no one wants to say anything. Now the meeting is over and everyone finds that not only did you not accomplish anything you set out to, but now you'll have to schedule a part two of the same meeting. It's pretty similar to when you go to the grocery store for bread, milk, and eggs and an hour and a half later, you've got all of aisles 7, 8 and, 9 in your shopping cart. But when you arrive home, you realize you forgot the three things you originally intended on purchasing. This is why making a list is critical not only to your grocery shopping, but to holding meetings as well.

The ideal agenda is one that is:
- **Sent in advance**, so as to allow attendees to gather their thoughts and materials prior to the meeting.
- **Concise and to the point**. No one wants to be a part of a meeting, where the agenda looks like the *Declaration of Independence*.

If someone within your organization does happen to call a meeting without submitting an agenda to everyone in advance, try to get in touch with whoever is holding the meeting and confirm whether or not you have any deliverables for the meeting. Either way, do your best to get yourself out of this meeting. Find alternatives like presenting your points to your manager in a two- to three-minute conversation in his or her office.

The goal is to free up your time. Being included in meetings doesn't necessarily mean you're important. On the flip side, being excluded from meetings doesn't mean you're *not* important. When the end objective is to drive towards solutions, and you happen to be able to solve it without a meeting…that's pure gold.

The point we're trying to make here is that meetings have the potential to waste your time; they keep you from finishing the things on your to-do list. After all, if you are in a meeting for 2 hours, guess what you aren't doing: your work. If you find other ways of getting your deliverables delivered without having to cut into your work time, then you will have saved yourself from a long meeting—and you will also get to go home at 5 o'clock!

Simply speaking, focus and stay on task in order to get the overall product you desire. Unproductive meetings beget unproductive products and outcomes.

All Work, No Play

We live in an age of social networks. And as much as we hate to say it, our millennial generation has a *major* addiction to Facebook, Twitter, Instagram, and YouTube. Because, who doesn't want to look at cat memes all day? I'm sure some of you may have experienced that tiny voice over your shoulder taunting you, saying "log in, log in, the pics from the party last night are posted!" You may even want to engage in a few tweets, because it's only 140 characters, which makes it quick, right? Work is work, however, and your number one priorities are your projects and objectives for that day. Does this mean you shouldn't log in at all? We'd argue there's nothing wrong with an occasional 5-minute break. We're not robots. But please recognize there is a problem when you're hitting "refresh" every five seconds just to see if your friend has replied to your last message! It's addictive, we know; just make sure you snap back out of your little fantasy world and get back to work! #WorkHardThenPlayHard.

Well... Maybe Some Play

One of the primary reasons people don't get as much work done as they could in a day is because they don't schedule time for breaks. Taking a 5-minute break every hour or a 10- to 15-minute break every 2 hours is good for you. Why do you think some companies have break areas? It's important for you to give yourself time to daydream, look at Facebook, Tweet, and vent to your friend about how Susie Smith in accounting is really working a nerve. What you'll find is that if you give yourself time to *not* think, you will have more quality thoughts when you're working that are actually related to the job you are supposed to be doing.

Procrastination of the Nation

Let's not forget the infamous "P" word. Yep... *procrastination*. Do you get a "rush" when your back is against the wall? Ever feel like you do your best work when you're crunched for time?

Heard it all before, and in some cases we would agree that procrastination can sometimes act as a catalyst for producing great work. The key word is "sometimes." Procrastinating every single day you go in to the office is a sure formula for failure. This isn't high school; the days of whipping up an essay the night before and actually getting a decent grade are long gone. When you take on more responsibility, and actually have multiple assignments that just happen to be due around the same time, one of them will ultimately fall through the cracks if you continue to "put it off."

I think we all know that the first step to recovery is to admit you have a problem. Go on; we won't tell anyone. Let's be real, we all procrastinate from time to time. There are certain things you can get away with at the last minute, and there others that you need to prepare for well in advance.

Let's take Stephanie, for example. Stephanie is a business analyst for a top luxury jeweler. Her job consists of reviewing and analyzing competitive business cases, conducting live research with consumers, and analyzing internal business sales data, among other things. Her manager wants her to get out of her comfort zone and bring her reports to life, so she gives her the opportunity to present in front of senior management. As an analyst, Stephanie is well-versed in running data and providing analytics to the team on a weekly basis. However, she hasn't had much practice with presenting, much less presenting to senior management. This moment is where Stephanie will decide what her strengths and weaknesses are. She already knows that she's a data "guru," and analyzes figures and reports six ways from Sunday. On the other hand, she also knows that she's been given a new responsibility and will need to brush up on her presentation skills and learn how to summarize all her main points into a solid, compelling, yet compact presentation. What can Stephanie afford to procrastinate on? You guessed it! It takes Stephanie only a small amount of time to pull sales data, analyze and report to the team weekly. She has mastered her own system with regards to reporting. However, Stephanie should certainly build in time each day to work on perfecting a solid presentation, since we've already discovered that's an area for improvement. Should Stephanie decide that she will simply put her preparation on the back burner until the week of her presentation, she's bound for a royal screw-up.

No matter what your scenario, make sure that you *go for what you know* if you're going to procrastinate. If you've been given a new role or responsibility, you may need time to feel around and get some questions answered. With that said, don't wait until the 11th hour if you can't back it up with awesome outcomes.

De-clutter Your Whole Life

The lives we lead at home often work their way into the lives we lead at work. If you're constantly questioning why your work life is so stressful and every day seems so unorganized and chaotic, perhaps you should pick up a mirror. Take a detailed look at the life you lead. Is your house clean? Are the dishes piling up so fast that you have to dip into your paper plate stash? Do you have clothes strewn every place *but* the closet? Do you keep a calendar? While these questions may seem trivial, they do indeed directly correlate with how organized or unorganized your life may be. A personal change requires a lifestyle shift beyond the cubicle.

Have you ever heard the phrase "take care of home"? Truer words haven't been spoken, and it all goes back to laying the foundation first. De-clutter your personal life and you may begin to see the effects of productive and less stressful work days.

Perform a Self-Evaluation
There is an old saying, "Every time you point a finger at someone, just remember there are three pointing back at you." Everyone is so eager to play the blame game and point fingers, but sometimes the problem lies with you. Just like a regularly scheduled oil change, we recommend you evaluate yourself and your work behaviors on a regular basis. Try not to be biased, and give yourself an honest review. Ask yourself a couple of the following questions to get started. Did you meet all of your deadlines? What was the quality of your work? Are you a team player (when it applies)? Do you procrastinate? Is it always someone else's fault but yours? Once you are finished with your self-evaluation, assess your strengths and

weaknesses. If you find that you are indeed on the right track and need a few minor improvements, your next bet is to start assessing the job, your co-workers, and your manager. Everything in this chapter is meant to provide simple and effective ways to keep your performance in first-rate shape. Quite a few of us like to blame others for our problems and our shortcomings. Rarely do we take the time and responsibility to figure out what we might be doing wrong. Self-examination is always the first place you should start in any dilemma, work-related or not. Know when the problem is you, and also know and trust yourself and your abilities to gauge when the problem is someone else. Throughout the course of this chapter, if you have found a few areas for improvement, now is the time to make appropriate adjustments. If, however, you have found that you have nothing to change or improve... we're calling you out; and it's probably time to step down from your super-sized pedestal and realize no one is perfect.

5

YOU: THE BUSINESS

"In all honesty, the only person you can change is yourself." Words to live by, from one of our favorite mentors. Now, when she said this, she was usually talking in the context of relationships, making sure we understood that you can't go into a relationship trying to change someone. If you wait long enough; the only one who ends up changing is you. We believe the same to be true in the workplace. If you think that your manager, co-workers, or anybody else is going to change, then think again. It's you who has to change. If you want to leave work on time at the end of the day, then you are going to have to make the change—and seeing you change, others around you will begin to adjust their attitudes, expectations, and their own work plan.

Start by treating yourself, your work, and your time in the office as a business. If a *business* is defined as a *provider of goods and services in exchange for money*, well guess what? You are a business.

So let's examine some basic principles of being in business, and see how they can be applied to your job.

7-Eleven

Ever wonder why your local 7-Eleven (or the equivalent) is so convenient? No matter what time of day or night, you can always count on getting what you want, when you want it, no questions asked.

Now, have you also ever wondered why your manager continues to pile project after project after project on you? Clearly it's because you're Wonder Woman or Superman and you can take on the world and all its problems with your mystical powers! No, it's because you're the 7-Eleven. Getting what you want when you want it works great if you're a brick-and-mortar convenience store, but employees who constantly have requests piling up (all of which are "URGENT") are going to feel the stress. Limits are the boundaries that keep the world in balance. When you step outside your limits, you run the risk of creating an imbalance in your work life and personal life. If you planned to get off at 6 o'clock, and end up getting off at 8; what happens? You're more than likely hungry (hangry in some cases), too tired to do anything fun, your favorite takeout place is closed, and your sleep schedule is altered. The next day, you're still mad about yesterday's chain of events, which is consequently causing a decline in your overall mood and productivity. All these situations could have been avoided if you knew your limits.

It's not your manager's fault that you didn't muster up the courage to say that you may need some help prioritizing all of his or her requests. No one can read your mind; if you want to set boundaries, you have to speak up.

As we touched on briefly in *Myths They'd Like You To Believe* (Chapter 2), all of the "connectivity" in the workplace can become daunting as you try to decipher where the rubber meets the road with work and personal life. Think your manager is going to hold your hand and create a color-coded work plan that separates work priorities and personal priorities for you? Well keep holding your breath and drowning in confusion, because we all know that is never going to happen. Truthfully, this isn't your manager's responsibility; it's yours.

Have you ever felt as though the concept of working and living life seems to be a little bit blurry? Have you ever stopped to ask yourself what your boundaries are? Perhaps the reason why you work until the wee hours is because you may not even know what your limits are. Take a peek at one of our personal stories below to see the ah-ha moment!

~Personal Anecdote from author Ashley Sutton~

When I first started working, I never took the time to determine my stopping point. I figured I was lucky to be there, so I'd better make it count. After I left my job where I was working unfathomable hours, it became clear to me, and I made a personal pact to figure out what my needs were. When I landed a position at another Fortune 500 company, I ended up having a totally different experience. This corporate culture was unlike anything I'd seen. My team was just as capable, hard-working, and all around rock stars, but they knew when to draw the line. I found that we were launching even more products than I was launching with my other job, yet I was less stressed, and quite frankly shocked that I saw sunlight on my way home consecutively. I will never forget my manager pulling me aside and asking me "what are you doing still here?" I stood there somewhat doe-eyed, because I honestly couldn't even answer her. I was so used to late nights that I literally think I was creating work for myself. I was working, but these were things that could have easily been put on the back burner for the next day, or even the next week.

I'm not even sure she knew it at the moment, but I literally had to start reprogramming myself from then on.

~~

Here's the solution: *set people's expectations appropriately.* How? Through your actions. If you stay at work late every evening for a week, in order to wrap up some newly-requested work (on top of your already-full list), then people are going to come to expect this from you every day, even if you only intended it to be temporary. Now your manager thinks that you can get 80 hours worth of work done in a 40-hour work week—your manager isn't noticing that you were working 80 hours to get it all done. And as we saw in the first chapter, *The Truth about Overtime*, your manager now comes to expect this every week, and all of a sudden your full-time job has become two full-time jobs for the price of one!

If you set the expectation with your supervisor that you don't work late, with the exception of special circumstances, then your manager will not come to expect 80 hours worth of work from you in a 40-hour work week. Conversely, if you set the expectation that you can get anything and everything done in a week, then you will continue to be asked to serve up the world on a platter in a week…..and it better not be late!

B2B

Business to Business transactions take place when one business provides services to another business— for example, a wholesaler and a retailer—in exchange for some form of compensation. Let's take Johnny's Wholesale Tire Company. Johnny sets up contracts and sells tires (in bulk) to various tire retailers across the nation. Do you think Johnny allows his customers (retailers) to come in and order tires at all hours of the day and night? I don't think so; Johnny has official business hours to provide services and fulfill orders.

Picture yourself as Johnny's Wholesale Tire Company and your employer as the retailer. You, the wholesaler, provide your services in exchange for a salary or wage from your employer (the retailer). Just as Johnny doesn't allow customers to make their own hours, you shouldn't allow your employer to make their own hours either. Does this mean come in the office at 9 a.m. and leave at 4 p.m.? Absolutely not; in fact it doesn't mean you should leave at any given time. It simply means that projects and assignments should be given a reasonable amount of time to be completed during the regular work day.

Become Valuable and Your Time Will Be Valued

This topic is vital to your success. Why? Because if you can get a good handle on it, you can become more effective, and in turn get one step closer to being successful. You'll stop working overtime, and start working in better time. You'll stop being underproductive and start producing better quality, and more than you could have imagined. Most important, you will stop giving your time away for nothing and start valuing *your* time. Most successful people are successful because they truly understand the value of their time.

If you want to be successful too, lean in and take notes.

Time is a resource, perhaps your most valuable resource because it is in limited supply. That's right, boys and girls, no matter how many top hats and bunnies you've got up your sleeve, you can't magically create more time. And it's not a natural resource, like oil; there is no place you can go to get more of it! It's very simple: there are 24 hours in a day, 7 days in a week, and 365 days in a year. That may sound like a lot of time, but if you break it down, you end up with only a fraction of that as "usable time." So let's take a step back and calculate how much time you really have in a day.

Start with 24, subtract 6 because that's how much you spend sleeping (on average). Now you have 18. Now subtract 2 because that's how much time you spend getting ready for work in the morning and for bed at night every day (we're not counting those 30 minutes you stare at the wall to wake up); that's 16. Take out the time you spend commuting to and from work, say, 2 hours, and you're down to 14 hours. Let's not forget the place where most of our life is spent…work. Most of us are set to work an 8-hour day, but end up working more. For the sake of this example, though, let's leave it at 8. Now you are left with 6. You haven't eaten anything yet, so unless you want to starve you should take out another 2 hours for breakfast, lunch, and dinner (if you are preparing these meals, you might need to subtract more). And then there were 4.

You are now down to four hours in a day that haven't been devoted to anything yet. But don't forget that you probably have personal things to take care of, errands to run, and groceries to buy. Also, if you planned on binge-watching on Netflix, you're going to need more than 4 hours; I mean come on! So after a full day's work, you only have 4 hours to spend doing what you want. Why would you choose to spend it working overtime and stressed out?

Here's what you have to do: get organized and utilize your time in a way that is most effective and beneficial to both you *and* your company. This means shutting down a few bad habits.

Stop Responding to Emails
Every day, all day, you probably get a bazillion emails from all kinds of different people asking you to do different things, and you probably stop each time you get an email to read it and respond. Stop doing this! First of all, you are interrupting your train of thought and slowing down progress on whatever project you are working on. Second, you will get emails all day long and most of them are not time-sensitive. If they are, wouldn't they warrant a phone call instead?

Make a conscious effort to create a schedule for

responding to emails. Some people prefer to answer priority emails first thing in the morning, and low to medium priority emails during the afternoon. That way you can focus on your work, instead of constantly interrupting it. Also, make others aware of that fact that you are doing this, so they adjust their behavior accordingly. Next time Michael in Finance wants to send you an urgent email, perhaps he will pop by your office instead.

You can also think of this in relationship to Johnny's Wholesale Tire Company. The core focus of his business is manufacturing tires and selling them to tire shops across America. While other things are important—like ensuring that coffee for the plant workers gets ordered every two weeks, or making sure that employees get uniforms with their names on them—nothing is more important than making and selling tires; and nothing comes before these two objectives are achieved. The same should be true for you at work. You have several items that you know you are responsible for as a part of your job. Those objectives should be achieved daily; then you can get to the other stuff.

Stop Helping Other People
We know it sounds harsh; hear us out. Imagine Johnny's Wholesale Tire Company on one of its busiest days of the year. Factory workers are working around the clock non-stop trying to produce a large number of tires for the release of a brand-new automobile that XYZ Motor Cars is going to release in a few weeks. As you may have guessed, Johnny's Wholesale Tire Company will be providing the brand-new tires to go on these brand new cars. So Johnny is going to be eating, sleeping, and breathing tires.

Now Bill, over at Bill's Tire Repair Shop, comes over to Johnny's Wholesale Tire Company and asks Johnny if he could assist him with making a large volume of tire repairs. Being that Johnny is in the business and all, Bill figures that Johnny would really be able to help him. Bill is right, in fact; Johnny *could* really help him. After all, he knows more about tires than anyone and can certainly tell you how to repair them good as new. So, here's the next question: what does Johnny do? Does he:

A.) Be a good neighbor and help out

B.) Tell him yes, but only after he has finished his big order

C.) Tell Bill to figure it out himself.

Let's discuss each option and determine which would be best.

Option A: Johnny agrees to help
If Johnny says yes to Bill, then he is going to have to stop production on his big tire order and begin working to help Bill. What does this mean to Bill? Well, it means a whole lot. Getting help from Johnny is really going to

make Bill's day. It is going to help him make more money, satisfy his customers, and ultimately make him look like a real genius, because not only did he get the work done that he needed, but he didn't have to do any of it himself! What does this mean to Johnny? Well, it means that Johnny loses money because he isn't fulfilling his tire order. It also means that his customers will no longer be able to rely on him to produce what he says he can, which means they will probably go elsewhere for tire fulfillment. Johnny ultimately ends up losing his livelihood, though he has gained the eternal friendship of Bill. It's too bad friendship doesn't pay the light bill and put food on the table. This scenario is not a win-win situation.

Option B: Johnny agrees to help
So Johnny has said yes to Bill, with the caveat that he will help only after he has finished fulfilling his big order. What does this mean to Bill? Well, he is not as happy as he would

have been with Option A, but is willing to wait a little while to get what he needs. After all, someone else is still going to do the work and he knows that Johnny will do what he says. What does this mean to Johnny? Johnny has now added another project to his already intense workload. He already has an order of tires to produce quickly, not to mention another order after he finishes that one, but he has promised to get Bill's tires repaired in between, so now he's obligated. Again, this means that one of his customers is going to have to suffer a little bit and wait, which could lead to a similar situation that he faced in Option A: loss of business. Though, this option is much more optimal than A.

Option C: Johnny tells Bill to figure it out himself
Johnny has decided to tell Bill that it's time to fend for himself. What does this mean to Bill? Well, it means that Bill is going to have to find another way to get his objective achieved.

He will probably either learn how to fix the problem himself or he will try to find another person to lay his problems on. What does this mean to Johnny? It means that Johnny only has to focus on his tire fulfillment, which is what he is in business to do in the first place. It means that his customers will get what they want when they want it, which means that Johnny can get what he wants: a successful tire business and happy customers.

The moral of the story is that it is absolutely fine to help out on occassion, but you can't get in the habit of doing other people's work for them. Read that again please. You simply can't go around helping everybody in your team or in your department with the work they have to complete. In this dramatic scenario, you are Johnny and everybody else is Bill. Bill may have work to get done, but that work has nothing to do with the work that you have to do. At the end of the day, you are in the business of doing whatever it is that you were hired to do. Those responsibilities should be outlined somewhere for you by your manager or Human Resources. Your customer is the company you work for. If you don't produce the service that you were hired to deliver, your customer will not be happy and will not want to continue being your customer. Either that or you will have to work overtime to ensure that you fulfill the orders your "customer" has made in addition to the request that your co-workers have made. The simple solution to this is to simply tell others no, in a respectful and professional manner. If they need help trying to figure something out or want you to complete a task for them, your answer could look something like this: "sure thing; however, I have a few priorities on my plate today and tomorrow, and am happy to help on [insert your feasible day/date here]." You weren't hired to do their job, and if they aren't efficient enough to figure out how to do their work, then that is not your concern (unless it's a team-wide deliverable). Your concern is producing the deliverables outlined to you in your job description, *punto final!* (that's Spanish for "point blank"). If your work isn't finished, your manager is not going to care that you helped Michael in Finance finish his work up. It's not even going to matter that you helped Brian in Marketing get his reports done. Your manager is only going to see that you did not complete what you were supposed to finish.

Of course, many of you would never let your supervisor see that you didn't complete your work. Instead, you'll just stay late helping Michael and Brian finish whatever it was they needed help with and end up working overtime; once again, not getting paid for it. This is unnecessary work and an absolute waste of your time and energy. Again, if Michael and Brian can't get their work done, let them explain that to their manager. Meanwhile, you get to go home and enjoy the rest of your day!

Be On Time

When Johnny decided to open up for business several years ago, he didn't have the luxury of really deciding his business hours. He saw that many of his competitors were open between the hours of 8 a.m. and 5 p.m. If he wanted to see any customers, then he knew he was going to set his business hours to match theirs. What's more, Johnny sticks to those hours and is always at work on time. He is never late because he might miss a sale, or not produce all the tires that he needs to produce in any given day. Needless to say, being on time is extremely important to Johnny's success.

Being on time for work should be extremely important to you, too. *When you are late*, not only does your manager see it, but you'll have to make up that time at the end of the day when everyone else is going home. *When you are late*, things tend to not get done the way that they should because you are rushing to catch up with everyone else. *When you are late*, you are usually frazzled and don't get your best work done. So, be on time. The more on time you are, the more work you can get done; and the easier it is for you to get home at a decent hour.

Be Disciplined

[**Discipline**]: *activity, exercise, or a regimen that develops or improves a skill.*

Johnny is an entrepreneur who owns a successful tire wholesale company. He has built this small empire from the ground up with his bare hands. Day in and day out, he committed himself to making his dream of a tire company a reality and today is reaping the benefits of that dream. He sells tires to businesses all over the world and reaps the financial benefits of those sales. How did he get to this point? One word: *discipline.* He worked every day, completing the necessary tasks to make his business a success.

Every day. That's what discipline is all about. It's about being committed to something day in and day out.

It's also about performing that same redundant task whether you really want to or not. Most people have in their heads, for some reason, that in order to do something day in and day out you have to thoroughly enjoy it. Nope. In fact, most of the time, discipline requires that you do something consistently that you sometimes don't want to do at all (assuming you're passionate about the overarching goal). For example, do you really think all gymnasts want to get up in the mornings and work out every day or miss parties with friends for fun? We're sure some would rather indulge in cakes and pies and lounge on the sofa (like the rest of us) instead of getting up to do cardio and crunches, but if they don't get up in the morning and workout, they won't have high energy or be fit. Gymnasts eat right and exercise so that they can continue to enjoy a successful career, which requires a healthy and fit lifestyle. You'll find that the most successful people in the world have the greatest amount of discipline. For the sake of time and argument, here are just two: Beyoncé and Mark Victor Hansen.

If you have been living anywhere in the world in the last 10 years, you have surely heard the name Beyoncé; and while she may certainly be a talented performer, it is fair to say that talent alone is not what got her where she is. Yes, there are many singers and performers all across the globe, but there is one thing that separates her from the rest: discipline. Discipline is the reason she is a world-renowned singer and performer and others are not. In the countless interviews that Beyoncé has done throughout her career, she always cites discipline as one of her keys to success. From the time she was little, she was out performing and singing at every opportunity she got, even if the venue wasn't appealing. Even now as a successful artist, she spends hours rehearsing her dance routines for her shows and managing a number of lucrative businesses. It is quite probable that Beyoncé doesn't get much sleep, and while she would probably rather be relaxing, she instead pushes herself to work harder than others with her same gift. That's just one of the many reasons why she's successful and others aren't.

You may not have heard of Mark Victor Hansen, but you may have heard about his books, or maybe even given one to someone as a gift. Mark is the co-author of the line of books entitled *Chicken Soup for the Soul*. If you can imagine for a moment what it takes to go from a simple idea to a book that appears in bookstores across the globe, then you will have an idea of why discipline is not fun. It requires writing the book, editing the book, reviewing the book, re-editing the book, reviewing the book again and again until it is a finished product. Not to mention locking in marketing plans and distribution channels. If you think that's fun, think again. Yes, writing a book is fun….for the first five minutes. After the initial excitement wears off, you are left with the reality that you have another 200 pages to write before you can even begin to get someone to look at it. This is where discipline comes in, which is exactly where Mark Victor Hansen and his partner succeeded. They did whatever it took, staying up hours on end to get *Chicken Soup for the Soul* finished. Did it pay off? Yes it did, and in a big way; to date the Chicken Soup for the Soul line of books has more than 100 million copies in print in over 54 languages around the world.

So if you want to be successful and successfully leave work on time every day, you are going to need to be disciplined, too. Now these two examples are examples of extreme discipline paying off in extreme ways. This is not meant to turn you into the world's next multi-platinum recording artist or a best-selling author; the point is to help you understand how important discipline is for you in your career. You don't need to be that extreme in order to be successful at what you do at work or to get home on time, but you are going to need a certain level of discipline. Day in and day out, just like Johnny, you are going to have to commit yourself to getting work done efficiently and remember that it's not always going to be sunshine and rainbows. There are going to be times when you will want to hop on Facebook instead of working, or chat with Carl about the latest piece of celebrity gossip. There will even be times when you will just want to daydream. Try not to do it. Remember the pain of working late and not getting to go home and have any leisure time. It is also the only way that you will climb the ladder of success. Be disciplined or be doomed.

6
INVEST IN YOURSELF

Let's talk about our friend Johnny, the tire entrepreneur again. Do you think Johnny was so successful because all the tools needed to build his business appeared out of thin air? You think customers started floating in with no marketing efforts? Do you think he began to form and maintain great relationships with car manufacturers because a fellow competitor was oh-so generous and thought he might need a helping hand with a few contacts, seeing as though he was new to the business? No. Johnny became successful not only because of his skillset, self-discipline, determination, and focus; but also because he invested in himself, and thus in his business. Every business needs the proper investments in order to function properly, whether it's investments of money, time, or any other resource.

Why do we bother investing? If we have some goal or goals in mind that we want to achieve, we set aside funds for it (be it stock, real estate, a new company) and hope to realize a good return. Why, then, should we not make the same efforts at self-investment in order to realize a positive return on our lives? Self-discipline doesn't just get handed to you on a silver spoon; you must work hard at it. It takes time, patience, and stick-to-it-ive-ness, all of which are valuable investments.

Successful people invest in themselves. Invest in the business of you. Here's how you can invest in you:

Change Your Mindset, Change the Game
Understanding your situation and changing your mindset is the key to becoming more successful at work (whether you work for yourself, or at a company). You must truly take the time to make a personal commitment to change your situation.

When architects design the next great structure, they start with an overarching idea. Once there's a clear direction, the process of drafting specs, blueprints, and so on can begin. It doesn't take a rocket scientist to know that you have to lay the foundation before you start building the house. We don't care how updated your AutoCAD software is; it all starts with a vision. In order to actualize the goal, you have to see it, map it, and go get it (and yes, in that order).

Start by adopting the three P's: **P**romise, **P**lan, and **P**erpetuate.

Promise

Actually write down a promise to yourself. Our minds work in mysterious ways. Once we begin to write down commitments (yes, with paper and pen) to ourselves, our minds process these visual cues and help us become subconsciously aware of where we want to be, thus moving us closer to our goals. Change can come in small consistent phases, but it all starts with determining how meaningful the change is to you, and promising yourself a positive outlook.

Plan

Now take your personal promise and begin to brainstorm or outline how you plan on getting the most out of your time at work. This sort of planning isn't your run-of-the-mill checklist. It's a plan created by you and for you. You will gain as much out of it as you put into it. Try writing a "From-To" plan, which ideally would compare your current work behaviors (where you're coming *from*) to your desired ones (where you want to go). Once you've identified the gaps in between, jot down the next steps you need to take to change those behaviors.

Examples:
- Constantly checking your phone for Whatsapp updates, the latest tweets, etc? Try keeping your phone on silent, turning off notifications, or placing your phone in your work bag, instead of in front of you at your desk. Even though it may seem like only a few minutes…those minutes add up. Before you know it, you could have spared yourself an extra 30 to 45 minutes (or more) total in a day.
- If you find yourself checking emails every

five seconds, as we mentioned in the previous chapter, try creating a set time to read and respond to emails (unless highly urgent). The best time to do this is probably at the very beginning and end of each day, depending on what your typical schedule is.

- If you currently step outside for a coffee break more than twice a day, perhaps you could think about limiting your coffee intake, see what's causing your "need" to drink coffee, or simply walk to the coffee machine in your office. You might even save some money while you're at it!

Creating solutions doesn't have to feel like pulling teeth. Find a specific problem and simply work toward fixing it.

Perpetuate

Have you ever made a New Year's resolution to get in the gym and stay fit? The first day you probably walked into the fitness club with a sense of purpose, as if you could take on the world. The next day you still felt that sensation. By the next week, though, you were probably not as motivated because your body got used to your routine and you don't see the results you desire yet. So, you slowly but surely stopped going. The gym is a place where only you decide your fate—no teacher to help you (unless you have a personal trainer); no friend to uplift you; just you. Unlike your New Year's resolution, don't allow your personal promise and self-preparedness to go to waste. It's up to you to keep the momentum going and perpetuate your new way of thinking.

It's true what they say, change is often one of the most difficult things to accept; but once you do, you'll never look back. Change your mindset, and you'll change your outcomes…it's just that simple.

How else can you invest in yourself? Let's take a look.

Pick a Project

If you only have one project that you constantly work on every day, you're in a silo and probably wasting your talent; get out of there while you can, if you can. If you're an employee who has the opportunity to grow and develop, however, you probably have various projects and tasks that you're constantly working on every day.

It's only natural to want to tackle all of your projects in one day, but be realistic about what you can really accomplish. If you have been given the opportunity to work on a few major projects that call for digging deeper than usual, require much more detail, and will help you develop and grow, you more than likely want to make them your best work ever. Palms start sweating, nerves become racked, and all of a sudden nothing on your daily to-do list seems important, because you're going in circles wondering how you're going to deliver on multiple projects or presentations while simultaneously making sure that your daily objectives don't fall through the cracks.

Find the solution. Try to pick an hour or two each day to devote to one special project or presentation, if possible. Literally block off time on your office calendar, be it Gmail, Outlook, or whatever calendar you use, and crank out your work. No phones (unless it's urgent), no mindless conversations, no BS. Continue to work like this and you will have more time to devote to fine-tuning vs. cramming and compiling. They didn't build the Empire State Building in one day; and you will probably not achieve the optimal outcome on the first round, either. Pacing yourself allows you to take time to step back from your work and rework, until you come to a place where you feel it's great work!

Stick to Your Guns

Toward the end of Friday's workday you probably start preparing for Monday's action plan on a sheet of scrap paper, or you even take it up a notch and track all tasks and projects using the latest and greatest project-management programs. Then Monday creeps up and the requests start flowing in. Just like that, your day went from perfectly planned to chaotic. By the time you've crossed out, redlined, and even drawn arrows all over your beautifully crafted to-do list, it's starting to look a lot like mindless scribble scratch.

Make certain that the items you're shifting around are indeed replaced with urgent or time-sensitive projects, and that they're producing outcomes that are directly relevant to your function. You took the time to plan your work for the day based on all upcoming projects, meetings, and day-to-day tasks, and therefore you should make conscious decisions regarding what's important to add to your plate, and what can wait, in order to get your work done.

We've said it before, and we'll say it again: the "help factor" is often one of the fatal flaws with prioritizing at work. Everyone wants to maintain a great rapport with their co-workers, and you should certainly go above and beyond for your team members, as you're all working toward the same goal. Sometimes, however, "maintaining great rapport," gets misconstrued as "I can always call so-and-so." It's great if they consider you knowledgeable and trust your opinion; it is also a major distraction if you're in the middle of projects. The "I just have a quick question," and the "this will only take a few seconds" will often sidetrack you for a big chunk of time, despite how harmless it may appear. Answering every question, putting your work on hold, and ultimately not completing your objectives for the day will put you way behind.

Helpful Hint: If you find yourself with a request that's not as urgent as one of your key priorities of the day, politely ask the requestor *when* they need the information. Explain that you may not be able to get to it that day, but you can certainly provide it the next day. Of course, if it's an urgent request, you'll just have to suck it up and buckle down. Otherwise, your first response should be to put it off.

Stick to your guns; if you continue to be a "Yes-Man" you will continue to inundate yourself with work that you know very well you will not be able to deliver. At the end of the day you are being evaluated on your work (not everyone else's).

Make a Judgment Call

I'm sure we all remember the fable of *The Boy Who Cried Wolf*. It's an age-old tale that can apply to many situations, *including* the workplace. Ever had a supervisor who just created difficult situations out of thin air? Most people aren't even aware that they create false alarms. A friend of ours, for example, reported to a manager who made certain assignments seem much more intense than they really were. Managers may not exactly understand the ins and outs of your daily tasks or your processes. Therefore, when a request rolls across their desk, they may begin "diagnosing" the situation before bringing it to your attention and getting your buy-in. Before you know it, you'll have a ridiculously robust request in your inbox that may not be the most optimal way to complete the assignment. However, this is your manager, so you oblige and follow instructions, putting all your other assignments on pause—and oh, by the way, this "request" has now taken an additional two hours to complete than it would have if it had been better planned by your manager.

Ask yourself if your manager fully understands the request before you begin wasting time and energy that you know (without a doubt) is unnecessary. If you know that an assignment requires certain inputs and should only take a certain amount of time, speak up! Your managers aren't perfect, no one is, and even they can sometimes overanalyze a situation. It's your job to gauge the request and give your honest opinion about the steps to complete it. Isn't that one of the reasons they hired you?

Accomplish and Leave
Once you've accomplished all the objectives you set out to accomplish for the day, it's time to do the unthinkable and actually go home. But unfortunately, when we finish our work, a sense of pride rushes over us and we tend to want to *continue* getting things done that very same day. It's a curious psychological phenomenon. Have you ever begun wrapping up your

work and then decided to check your inbox? What about checking that voicemail indicator that's been blinking since late afternoon? You don't check into these things because they're urgent; you check into them because you're *curious*. The next chain of events is pretty predictable. You'll start working on a request and justify it by telling yourself, "oh it's easy, it won't take too long," or "I'll just do it tonight so that I won't have to worry about it tomorrow." Then as Murphy's Law would suggest, what should take 5 minutes takes 30 minutes or longer, or your computer crashes. Now you say to yourself "well, I already started, so I might as well get it done." And inevitably you're now working to the sound of crickets and missing another evening at home or out with friends.

Question: Do you honestly feel that if you get through all your emails every single day, you won't have the same crowded inbox the very next day? *Answer*: I think you already know the answer! Reality Check: the work will always be there, and there's nothing you can do to change that. What you can do is continue to map out your daily objectives and meet them. Continuing to pile on extra work is like going back to the buffet too many times: it's irrational and will only make you sleepy!

Your work patterns and habits are determined by you. You can continue to live by them or you can change them. No one said it would be easy, but without a clear vision of what you want, you can't expect to improve your situation. Challenge yourself to really go that extra mile and make a commitment to enjoy work while at work, but also to enjoy life outside your cubicle. Most people don't see the end of the race until they're approaching the finish line. Try visualizing the finish line when you lace up your track shoes, before the race even begins.

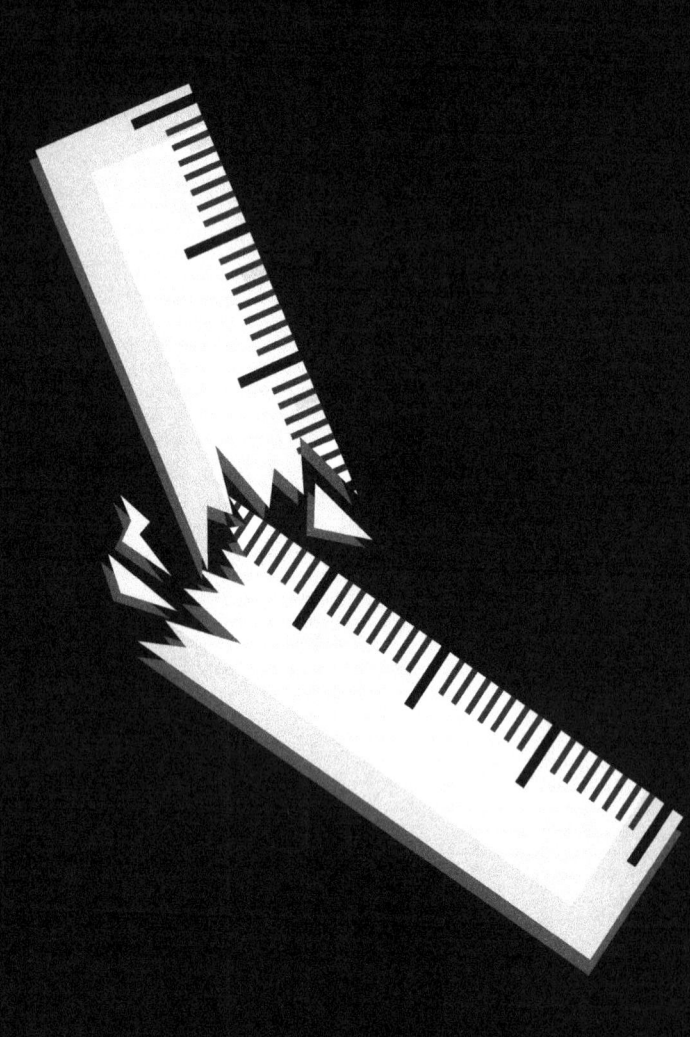

7

EXCEPTIONS TO THE RULE

You wouldn't waste time in a job you didn't at least like, right? If you're feeling overwhelmed and frustrated, that doesn't mean you hate your job. It just means you have to find that happy medium and get control of your work behaviors. Here and there you will surely need to burn the midnight oil, but when it becomes a habit, it's time to make a change.

I'll have a Mai Tai and a...budget report?
Picture yourself on one of the beautiful Maldives islands, basking in great weather, sipping on a Mai Tai (or any libation of your choice), and having a massage so good you feel like you're floating. You then float back to your suite and prepare for bed when and all of a sudden your room phone rings. Guess who? It's your supervisor (only 8,000+ miles away), and he's freaking out because there's a presentation the week you return, and come to find out, there are a hefty amount of revisions to your piece of the presentation to complete. This leaves you only a day or two to complete the revisions once you return.
Redbull...check. Laptop...check. Backup work files...check. Vacation....down the drain!

Now it's time to trade in your Mai Tai for a Venti espresso. You start cranking away at the last few bits of information necessary for the presentation. You're working in a different time zone than your counterparts, so you'll have to send your questions, comments, and drafts first thing in the morning in order to get a response by that evening. After a few cups of coffee, back and forth emails, and maybe a Skype video conference, you're done with your inputs and feel confident about that upcoming presentation. Whew! Now it's time…to pack? You only have one day left on vacation. Don't forget to catch up on your Z's during the plane ride, because it's back to work tomorrow morning.

The moral of the story, my friends, is that unless you want to work in Excel and PowerPoint during your vacation, you better make sure you tie up any loose ends before you step foot on that plane, or whatever method of travel you're taking. A friend of ours unfortunately had to learn the hard way. He was super amped about this one über important presentation and prepared his butt off (or at least he thought he did). An hour or two before the trip, he had to edit and re-work his entire part of the presentation. He was torn between making his trip on time and making last-minute corrections to the presentation. So, like any overzealous fresh graduate, he decided to multitask and finish the work on the way to his destination. Bright idea, right? We think not!

As he was cranking out his final edits and additions, the wireless connection crashed. All of his data was lost, and the presentation wouldn't save because the file was too large. He ended up having to send an email to his managers to let them know he wouldn't be able to make the deadline. It was the worst email he'd ever had to send. He'd let the team down. Needless to say, his "vacation" didn't feel like much of a vacation because his mind was focused on his first *major* screw-up. When it comes to time off, you should:

A.) Plan ahead and make sure you get the necessary "stamps of approval" before you duck out, or

B.) Try not to plan a vacation around the time of a major project.

We all deserve a vacation. But don't discount yourself or your team by not finishing your work. Wouldn't you rather be stressed about those "mysterious" back-to-back charges from the hotel bar on your AMEX bill?

Short Term vs. Long Term

"Not going anywhere for a while?" This should not be your tagline when you think about work. By all means, we believe in achieving and taking the necessary steps to get ahead, produce awesome work, and ultimately find your niche at your company. But the aforementioned can be achieved without going into delirium every single night. Let's not put truth to the saying "you are your work." We'd much rather you be praised for your work rather than the number of hours you penciled in on your timesheet.

If you really find it hard to wean yourself off those late nights at the office, you should make a pact to stay late on select days of the week. Take a look at your personal commitments outside of work. For example, if you have fitness goals, the weekend may not be enough time to devote to your objectives. The gym has great classes during the week, which can help with dedicating a set time to physical activities. So, if you know your cardio kickboxing class starts at seven o'clock in the evening every Tuesday and Thursday, these would probably be the best days for you to stay later at work so you can simply leave work, head to the gym, and then head straight home. Alternatively, if you're craving a night out and typically hang out with your crew on a Friday night, you should certainly make a conscious effort to get out of the office on Fridays in time for happy hour specials!

The Big Catch

Bait it, hook it, and reel it on in! These are the most universal words of any fisherman. What makes a fisherman successful? Is it luck? Is it being in the right place at the right time? While the latter might ring some truth, successful fishermen are great because they have all the right materials to make the catch. They are disciplined, and they have mastered the basics of fishing.

We've previously mentioned that staying late won't get you that lovely promotion or recognition you've been vying for, but in some cases it does pay off. Once you begin mastering your daily roles and responsibilities, you'll probably start to notice more free time, and thus want to take on more. If your manager is familiar with your work style, he or she will probably notice you twiddling your thumbs and realize that you're ready to take it up a notch. Even if your manager doesn't initiate a new project for you…ask for it! Next thing you know, you'll be jumping into your next big catch. Just like the fisherman, it's all about the right materials, discipline, and making sure you have your basics down pat. Remember, with every new opportunity comes added responsibility.

A new project could most certainly be a great stepping stone to a promotion, assuming you meet the expectations of your manager. This may sound easy to do; but remember you must maintain your daily roles and responsibilities in addition to tackling your new role, without slacking on either. When you first start out, you may have to put in a few extra hours a week. Your great ability to juggle the day to day, coupled with discipline and dedication to your new role will more than likely be key influencers when your managers are deciding who should be considered for a promotion and/or a raise.

Team Player

While it is important to be known as a self-starter and an employee who follows through, it's also important to be a great team player. Again, let's not mix up being a team player with letting everyone dump their work in your lap. Definitely not; the kind of team work we're talking about is when you and your co-workers have a huge presentation or project to prepare for, and everyone's burning the midnight oil together. After all, two heads are better than one. Besides, if you don't work together, we can assure you that your presentation, project, or whatever you're working on will not sound like a cohesive piece of work. Now why is that? Different trains of thought lead to different ways of writing, which lead to different interpretations, which can often, consequently, lead to a choppy and seemingly unorganized presentation. When you work as a team, everyone has the opportunity to work, re-work, and create a streamlined outcome. Some of you may be asking yourselves "why should I have to stay late if *my* part of the work is finished?" Good question; however, that's not the kind of attitude you should take with a *team* project. Assuming you're done with your part of the project, the reason you stay late is because this is a *team* effort, and one of your co-workers may actually need your help, have a question, or even want your opinion on a piece of the puzzle. Once the team feels the work is in a good place, by all means feel free to go home. Use your judgment wisely; there are some team members who can put a damper on everything. You know the ones I speak of. Nitpicky Nicholas always has something to say about every little thing and wastes time talking about what's wrong instead of focusing on how to make it right. We all know a Panicky Paul, who's always in a frenzy and super nervous about writing, saying, and even thinking the wrong thing. Let's not forget the Negative Nancy co-worker, who can't ever find a compliment about anybody's work (except her own). Keep an eye on these types of co-workers, or you'll never see your fluffy pillow until *they* feel you can leave.

Think of your work habits as a game of cards. Your everyday work schedule is your primary deck (Ace, 1, 2, 3, etc.). Working overtime should be your wild card or your joker; hence, it should not be played consistently. Play your overtime wild card only when it's really necessary.

8

THE END GAME

For those of you who were hoping to get the goods on what this book has to offer by flipping straight to the end, you have found the *Spark Notes* version of the book. Don't cheat yourself out of what could be the change you may need to find some balance in work and life. It all starts at page 1.

For those of you who had the gumption to read the entire book, congratulations! You have almost made it to the end, although we hope this will be just the beginning for you.

Throughout this book, we have discussed some of the causes of overtime, the problem with overtime, and some solutions to helping you keep overtime to a minimum. It is so easy to gripe and complain about how stressful our lives have become because of working overtime; but we must remember that we have the ability to change our situations, and it starts with a few key ideas.

The Truth about Overtime
- Adopt the happiness factor! Overworking can cause elevated levels of stress.
- Life is meant to be lived outside of the office.
- You begin to create a false sense of productivity, and devalue your salary when working overtime consistently.

Myths of the workplace

- Sometimes being connected to work 24 hours a day, 7 days a week on every device leads to being over-connected and over-worked.
- Piling on more work isn't a "growth opportunity;" it's more work, with the same amount of time in a day.
- People don't always notice or care when you stay late. Being the team member that stays late every night doesn't score you any major points.
- Doing other people's work, and neglecting your projects will show that you're a good team player---said no one ever.
- Working longer and harder doesn't always lead to a promotion.
- You won't always be acknowledged for your work. Learn how to deal with it.
- If your coworkers stay late every day, don't mimic this behavior. They're more than likely working inefficiently.

Maybe It's You

- Be honest with yourself. It's not your manager that's keeping you at your desk; perhaps it's you.
- Learn how to better prioritize.
- Always plan ahead.
- Stop tweeting, texting, and looking at hilarious memes every 5 seconds, when you should be working.
- Taking breaks is a MUST—learn when to take them.

You: the business

- Treat yourself as a business at work, and own it start to finish.
- Start valuing your time and your time will be valued.
- Be on time.

Invest in yourself

- If you want to change your current habits, you've got to adopt the 3 P's (Promise,

Plan, Perpetuate), and begin forming productive habits.

Exceptions to Overtime
- There are always exceptions in life, and the same goes for working overtime. Never leave the office with a critical project unfinished. Respect yourself, but respect your team by completing your piece of the work. Never leave anyone hanging.

(Psst...there's more; keep reading)

The most critical lesson of all is to <u>know your worth</u>.

Knowing your worth is empowering. Often we allow companies to determine our worth simply because they determine our paychecks. Don't allow your fancy benefits package and competitive salary define who you are. Any old company can slap a price tag on an employee, but only you have the power to determine your value. We encourage you to live a fulfilled life that minimizes unnecessary stress.

Once you know your true value, you will perform better at work, not allow others to take advantage of you, and your days of overtime will be so over.

THANK YOU

We only hope this book has encouraged and inspired you to take back the time you deserve. Life is meant to be lived. We truly want to hear your stories. Please feel free to drop us a note to Hey@Overtimebook.com and let us know how you've progressed.

We can't wait to hear from ya!

ADDITIONAL RESOURCES

VISIT US: www.OvertimeIsSoOver.com

As a thank you for purchasing this book, please use the QR code below for free guides on productivity in the workplace and many more exclusive freebies!

Even more resources available on the website!

ACKNOWLEDGMENTS

First and foremost, while it may sound cheesy, we'd like to thank YOU for taking a chance and picking this book up. We know everybody's got a million (and one) ways to leave work on time. You chose us, and we are eternally grateful.

To our moms, dads, family and friends that continue to be supportive on this journey-- we THANK YOU and LOVE YOU!

Thanks to Linda Carbone for editing this from dream to reality! We are so thankful.

And here's a thank you to the strangers that have no idea how much they helped us during the process...

Thank you to that co-worker (who shall remain nameless) who vented such a wealth of much needed inspiration for this book. Cheers to the late nights!

Thank you to the Starbucks Barista and the security guard at the Barnes and Noble on 82nd and B'Way; goodness... so.many.late.nights.

Thank you to an old manager who wisely said "it's not about how long you work; but about how smart you work."

Also, thank you to Alice's Tea Cup (Chapters I and II) for being an inspirational haven to write in solitude (pumpkin scone included).

Thank you to the woman on the train that let Ashley "borrow" that green pen; it helped me jot down the title for this book!

ACKNOWLEDGMENTS

Ashley's Personal Acknowledgments:

To my mother, Halcyon, who has been my rock through it all; thank you for helping me find my strength to live life to the fullest. Thank you for being there through the late nights and early mornings. Thanks for being the audience, the editor, the motivator and the cheerleader all wrapped in one. I couldn't have made it through this journey without you.

To my dad, Tony-- thank you for continuing to be a fighter in life. Thanks to both you and mom for always allowing us to tap into our creativity and our entrepreneurialism (even if it meant selling candy on the schoolyard). Thank you for showing me how to be resourceful; I am now ruler of the shoestring budget (haha)! #KeepYourExpensesLow

To my big brother, Rahmon-- where do I start. Words cannot express how much I love ya. Though we have been far apart, you've always had my back, and continued to lift me up, even when I couldn't. It's very rare that brothers and sisters have a tight bond like you and I, and I can only hope that it gets even tighter. Cheers to a new chapter in life; one filled with laughter, love, and success.

To my lovely aunt, Ada-- you are such an inspiration in my life. So vibrant, loving, and inspirational. You've always got my back. I love you to infinity and beyond. You are favored!

To my amazing family-- some of you may not have even known I was writing a book, but I assure you that your love has kept me going, whether you knew it or not. There were so many times I had writer's block, and even some doubts about launching this book, and seeing pictures and posts

ACKNOWLEDGMENTS

helped me remember why I do what I do (especially my cousin Sterling… #ImJustTextingOutLoud).

Sherrell, let's talk about it! Not only are you an amazing woman and friend; you are an ultimate motivator. Procrastination is a disease, and we both helped to cure one another, haha!! Seriously though, thank you for helping this book, and my dream come to life in more ways than one. You are a goddess.

Jane Gardner, you are so talented; I can't even. Thank you for bringing this vision to life with such awesome designs. I wish you continued success in your design career, and am so thankful our paths crossed.

Scottie, thank you for being so supportive of me during this book journey. You were among the first to read and review the book, and your feedback was invaluable. I continue to be so very proud of you and your real estate business, and have no doubt you're not finished yet!

Marida Curry, Amy Vance, and Brian Stephenson, thank you for being the first to read this book; it's always great to have people in your corner with a fresh perspective!

Faria and Linda, thank you for the continued check-ins on the progress of finishing this book up! I can always count on you to keep it real. More importantly, thank you for your friendship throughout this process.

Finally, thanks to everyone who believed in this project, and offered encouragement (knowingly or unknowingly) along the way!

www.ingramcontent.com/pod-product-compliance
Lightning Source LLC
LaVergne TN
LVHW041544070426
835507LV00011B/926